I Am Not a Poet, These Words Just Got Me Through

I Am Not a Poet, These Words Just Got Me Through

Trials, Tragedy, Triumph

T. Helene

T. Helene Publications • Milton, Delaware

Copyright © 2023 by T. Helene

All rights reserved.

No part of this publication may be reproduced, distributed, or transmitted in any form or by any means, including photocopying, recording, or other electronic or mechanical methods, without the prior written permission of the publisher, except as permitted by U.S. copyright law.

First paperback edition, 2023

Paperback ISBN:
979-8-9877809-0-9

First eBook edition, 2023

eBook ISBN:
979-8-9877809-1-6

Library of Congress Control Number: 2023933201

For permission requests, contact T. Helene Publications at thelene_1@outlook.com.

Author Photo by J. Arielle
Edited by Emilia Rivera
Book Cover by Sovereign Noir Publications
Interior Layout and Formatting by Sovereign Noir Publications

Dedication

This work is lovingly dedicated to the woman after whom I affectionately chose my pen name–Helene C. Polk. My grandmother. Gone but not forgotten. Her life lessons vibrate within me as her legacy whispers words of encouragement in times of trials and tragedy. During moments of triumph, I feel her smile within my heart as I remember the way she used to say, "I'm proud of you baby."

I also dedicate this book to my mom, Ms. Cooky. My ride or die. The one person on this earth that has always been in my corner, cheering me on. I pray to be half the mother you are.

I would be less of a wife and mom if I failed to thank my husband and kids. Thank you Jay, Josh, Janae, and grand pets (Billy & Tar) for being my reason for pushing. You are the best family a woman like me could have. Thank you for loving me unconditionally.

Lastly, my sister circle. Small but mighty. Where would I be without your support through the many seasons in my life? Evelyn, Rae, Krystal, Frannie, Natascha, Talisha, Missy, Yvonne, and Nancy. Without the purpose you each play in my life I know beyond any doubt I would not have made it through the tragedy or the trials.

Introduction

The concept for this book manifested through my feeble attempt to join a community-based writing group to take a stab at something I've always been passionate about without formal training, writing. Having very little background knowledge about poetry other than 10th grade lit class, I had this horrible tendency to rhyme entirely too much. For several years I experienced tragedy, trials, and triumph at a mind-numbing pace. It was because of the pressure I faced that I began to write and keep what I wrote, overly rhymed or not.

I want to tell you, through my writing, how I survived. I want to share my experience, strength, hope and tears with you. I want to help you realize that you too can survive the storms of life. I need to say I am better now. I trust myself now.

These Words Just Got Me Through

Broken Tiara

Crooked in thought
Perplexed in mind
My tiara glistened still
But rusted by time
Futile efforts
Dating caused pain
I didn't understand
Or even know the purpose of my reign
My throne was vacant
As I rummaged through dirt
Someone handed me a cloth
and showed me my worth
I began to polish hard
Bringing up pain
Uncovering scars
Releasing disdain
Purpose more clear
Value and destiny understood
My tiara shone brightly
My throne felt good
My mind transformed
My heart was set free

I am the prize
My empire lies before me
Freedom ain't free
I did my work
No more sifting through mud
Or finding frogs in dirt
I rule with love upon my thrown
Destiny revealed, purpose is known
Rise, curtsy and bow because now I am full grown

A Poem for Ray: The Struggle Is Real

I see you
I see your pride
I see your hurt as you're cast aside
I hear your voice
Anger and all
I answer the phone every time you call
Your story is deep
Feelings shallow
Your purpose unknown your own pity you wallow
Everyone is to blame
You are always the victim
I see you
I see your fear
I see your struggle and it is very real

Confusion

I keep trying to believe
Trying to love
Trying to be what you say you need
I keep hoping you have changed
Hoping you will refrain
Be true and loyal
See this love through
My heart hurts
My mind too crowded to think
I do not know what to believe
What to feel
What to think
It's just,
simply put,
Confusion

Companionship

"I like it too much to be
single the rest of my life," is the excuse
I whisper to myself, as I look into the mirror before yet another random
date.
I crave it,
Long for it,
Especially at night.
The yin to my yang.
Tall
Dark, handsome
Chocolate thang.
Precious
Sweet
Time with this man complete
Companionship

The Conversation

My palms began to sweat as I approached the door,
my body trembled in fear as I knocked
His voice, once soothing now evoked fear as he bellowed, "Who is it?"
"It's me. Can we talk?" felt like rocks in my throat as I responded.
His deep sigh welcomed me into the room I once enjoyed.
Now the air so thick with fear I could taste it as I sucked in a deep breath.
Upon exhale, the words rolled off my tongue "It's over. I can't do this anymore."
With each word, my courage grew;
With every syllable
my heart felt more free.
Years of being locked down, smothered, and stuck all led to this moment,
this one conversation;
my freedom loomed near.
His response, "Get out! Don't take anything, just go."
My response, "Yes, I will gladly do so."

Jailbird

In and out
In and out
Running routes
All for clout
Some would say
There is a better way
Looking over your shoulder
The streets are getting colder
Your life much older
It is time to let it go
Work towards something and let it grow
Slow and steady wins the race but
You running at an unsafe pace
Stay out the streets
Make something real
No more in and out time to cut a new deal
Cuz shit is getting real

Attention

I thrive with it
It feels so good
Makes me smile
Addictive
The high makes the world brighter
I lose it eventually
I must learn to live without it
The cycle will continue
Attention seeking behavior
The root of my woes
Loneliness, low self-esteem
My need for validation shows

Lucky Stars

Could it be
Is it real
Someone for me
Afraid to look deep
Shocked at possibilities
Feels right so far
Thanking my lucky stars

Pages

Blank
No ink
Must put thought to pen
Given this gift for naught
Lines,
upon lines,
swirling in my head.
I must get it out.
Maybe I should use lead...
Writer's block

Fear

Squeezes, grips, tighter still;
Lump in my throat;
The fear is real.
My GOD is bigger,
able to provide.
Nevertheless, fear haunts me,
It badgers my pride.
I know I will make it
We will be okay
Regardless of what Washington D.C. has to say

The Wall

It is present;
big but vague at the same time.
Honesty says,
fear and this wall are intertwined.
Could it be my schedule,
lack of sleep or time,
or fear of failure;
This wall feels too steep to climb.
I used to be willing,
fear never shook me,
now I wonder will I let this wall beat me.
So, I fight back,
as I always do.
Put pen to paper with hopes it will demolish the fear.
Here's to my breakthrough from writer's block being near.

In Peace

The lights all twinkle,
the halls are decked,
but the void in my heart,
leaves my shirt and cheeks wet.
I try to be happy,
and smile real big,
but without you here,
some things just don't make sense.
Your smile infectious,
your laugh echos,
your lap I miss terribly,
your voice so mellow.
Your cakes and pies,
jokes and humor,
so hard without you,
I must get stronger.
Our love eternal,
your grace you left.
We will meet again.
Till then, just rest
In peace.

Deep

Our feelings are deep,
our hearts are full
to capacity,
how can I ever love you more?
A love so real,
understood by neither,
treading in deep waters,
the abyss swallows me.
I tilt my head back
to breathe.
Gasping for air,
I suck in your scent,
love grows deeper and deeper still,
it is all so surreal.
Meeting only by chance;
A coffee, black, atm
and one deep glance

Quite unexpected
Quite by surprise
Instantly tears formed in my eyes
A deep breath I took
My voice and hands shook
As I asked the results
Grabbed this pen
Prepared myself, maybe not
More tests required
My hands and phone hot
I will get through this
My heart just sank
My life forever changed
By this call

When You Hold Me

When you hold me, all stress melts away
In your voice, the Sun shines bringing the dawning of a new day
In your smile, I see forever, the future, my plans and love
HIS will complete like a hand in a soft, warm glove
When you hold me, all my dreams manifest
The hurt, pain and fear my heart can no longer possess
Just hold me.
Now that you hold me, my heart skips a beat
My mind so at ease, my days more complete
When you hold me, HIS love rings true in you
Nothing missing, nothing broken, is how HE made you
Keep holding me
Do not let go
Please hold me and let's watch this love grow

Tears fall
Choked up
Your presence heals
All fears dissipate
Under your hand
Your touch heals

Look To The Hills

I look to the hills
Here comes my help
My help comes from the Lord
If I'm on the mountain
Or in the valley
My God will be with me
As HE never sleeps.

Missing You

I miss the way you smile
How we used to drive for miles and miles
Your touch so gentle
Voice so sweet
I miss all you did with me.
A ghost from the past
Love that did not last
A haunting of memories
Your voice calling out to me.
Could it all be in my mind?
Could I see you materialize in just the nick of time?
Maybe it's not meant to be
Maybe you're not missing me
Could there be a one for me,
Or just a figment, wish or distant memory?
Could I bear this pain once more?
Should I open this door?

But You

Texts, hang ups and random hoes
Promise me this ain't the way love goes
My heart's all open, my tears flow too
But nothing matters to me but you
Nothing really matters but you
Two faces, two lives and multiple wives
My head starts spinning as I wonder why
My heart beats fast, fear multiplies
Yet nothing matters to me but you
Nothing really matters but you
I should matter too

Well Done

When all is said
And all is done
I just want to hear "Well Done"
I want to know my work was not in vain
My pain led to promise
My lack to great gain
My days of endless trials
My nights of dark, unspoken pain
Was all worth entrance into your heavenly domain
Reunited with my loved ones
Your gates opened wide for me
Eternal rest in your presence
Forever relishing victory
Focused no more on earth, pain, sweat or tears
All distant memories
My soul persevered
Simply to hear "Well Done, you may enter"

Adsila, Rachael, The Way 3/31/2023
Ranu: Creative Developments, Los Angeles
www.ranutoday.com

Trust

So hard to build
So easy to break
I gave you my all
Still a fool you make
The games
The lies
Yet you stay and apologize
I am always to blame
Will it ever be the same
My heart beats slow
Wish I didn't know
Rather be in denial
Now gotta force this fake ass smile
Trust, you betray
My feelings insane
Yet you say you changed
so, I swallow the pain

Come Forth

Dead bones
Old things
All are made new
Come forth, come forth
All are made new
New mercies
New grace
All given to you
Come forth, come forth
All are made new

Elevator Crush

When the night falls, I long to hold you close
You are the only one I will ever need
Just please show up, come to me
Been looking for you at the mail slots
Even took the stairs
Longing for the love I could only dream of

I dress real cute, remain a dime
Hair slayed, walk a fine line
Smile real big, yet you ain't even here
Love is a bitch, infatuation only gets worse
You were my crush on the elevator,
and now you're gone, and it hurts
Missing your touch, how I dreamed it would feel
Missing your voice, that cute way you scratch your ear
Got ten toes down yet nowhere to stand round here
You've gone missing poof, moved on and disappeared

I gave you a chance
To love me right
To be here for me
Understand my plight
I gave you a chance
To be honest and true
I gave you a chance
To be the real you
The chance to be sincere
I thought our love was real
The dreams we aspired
But your chance sir
Has expired

By My Side

Winds can blow
Water rise
All I know is you are by my side
For rich or poor
No end in sight
Yet I have peace cause you are by my side
You calm the seas
The wind subsides
I smile cuz I know you are by my side
Peril lurks
Enemies encroach
Viruses spread
I won't dread I have hope instead
You never fail
You will prevail
Cuz you are always by my side

You Call My Name

You call my name and tell me you love me
I raise my hands and ask you for blessings
I close my eyes cause I know I'm not worthy
My hands unclean and my heart so dirty
But you call my name and tell me you love me
Choices I've made against all your guidance
My life unchanged cause of my pride
My words are few, tears overflowing
But you call my name and tell me you love me
When you call my name, life all makes sense
When you call my name, no more do I lament
Your voice calms my soul, your touch makes me whole

The Set Up

I listened
Tried to obey
I feel like I've been set up
The hopes I felt
The dreams I held
Hard to see it all
I feel like I've been
Set up
You said you would be different
Listen closely and understand
Seems more like you are the same exact man
Growth is optional and my feelings are too
I need you to be less like them and more like the real you
Don't make me feel set up

Anxiety

Jaw popping
Knee shaking
Heart racing
Narrow vision
Breathe, breathe, breathe
Relax
It's okay, you're okay, everything is okay
Breathe

Frustration

I keep trying, knowing my effort
Will lead to
frustration
My pride won't let me quit
The longing comes and I can't not
try
1, 2, 3, 4, here it comes once more
Frustration

Grief

Like a wave
Crashing, swirling
I fall back, off balance
Struggle for fresh air
My lungs burning from the longing
Heart racing
The wave comes
The wave goes
I'm still here to float along

The Itch I Can't Scratch

How do I describe it
The massive void you left
That can only be filled by your voice
I miss that soft rattle from your chest
and our weekly chats
The way you got loud to prove your point
Sports seasons fly by with me missing your input
My tears fall less, slower but still there
When I think of the day you left us none of it seems fair
The longing to hear your voice
Laugh with you some more
You leaning in the window, me standing on the porch
Truly the itch I simply can't scratch

It Started with A Game

Who knew we would be twin flames
Hopes of a little girl
Dreams of a little boy
You made me use all your broken toys
I teased you to no end
We truly did not know one day
We would be more then friends
Basketball, Two square and made-up games
I never imagined one day I'd take your name

The Morning Dew

Early I rise
Your grace fresh and new
Your purpose so clear
Like the morning dew
As the sun rises over a pasture
Gratitude I feel
Life is all anew
Birds chirp your praise
Your presence in the breeze
The flowers reach towards the heavens
There's praise in the trees
Your renewal is what I long for, so I wake early enough to see
The promises you left and the dew on the leaves

Careless Words

You speak so freely
Not missing a beat
Your words are careless
Leaves me questioning defeat
I feel you are the enemy
During times like these
Your words are your weapons
That cause me to bleed
Sorry I'll do better
Your best next line
Better won't stop the tears
That fell from my eyes
Careless words hurt every, single time

Sisterhood

We reach out
We truly care
We share our hearts
We agree to prayers
We laugh, we cry
We sing, we dance
Would raise our hands
To defend our stance
You're a part of me
And I of you
Common threads
Heart's desires too
Others come and go
Life spins on and on
But trials don't change us
Our connection stays strong
My sister

Sprinklers

No rhyme or reason
The fury comes quick
I get soaked by the assault
As my groggy day begins

Turning lemons into lemonade
Bringing back my inner child
I will eventually learn to laugh and play
If only for a little while

I stand still in the barrage
Of water jetting to and fro
Wet but smiling
Wondering if this is how the day will go

I Have To

I feel the push to participate
My mind, my schedule wants me to wait
The call still echoes deep within
Should I do it?
Should I pass?
Will I blow the chance for us to win?
Part of me wants to try
Part of me wants to hide
As I open the book
I can't help but think
I have to

My Neighbor

Opposites at first glance
Stopping to speak I took a chance
Oddly enough it was meant to be
We like the same bakery
And would've both taken a knee
We agree on so many thoughts
Enjoy thrifting and all
Made up new words in text
To describe laughing it off
Chats on the patio
As our perspectives grow
Glad I took a chance
This proves you just never know where friendships will grow
...my neighbor

Still Here

I wondered will I make it
Many long nights
Undiagnosed pain
The fear of death was very real
I wondered will I make it
Or will they find me lying here
I thought about my hopes
I prayed about my dreams
I cried out to you begging for relief
Another year has passed and I'm still here
Walking out your plan
Fulfilling your destiny
I'm still here

Different

I know you feel different
And it's okay
Your fear of me knowing
Is truly in vain
I love you no matter what
Will fight for you til death
I know you feel different
It's all so complex
But love is so simple
And flows freely from me to you
I know you feel different
Yet I remain judgment free
With open arms to hug you
Loving heart to help you run your race
I know you feel different
Please know I don't care
No matter who you love I will always be here
I know you feel different

Don't Hug Me

Don't hug me
Cuz it'll make me cry
I know you see the fear in my eyes
Don't hug me or hold me close
My nose will get stuffy
My head will hurt
Don't hug me
Cuz the tears will flow
I just don't understand why we all didn't know
Don't hug me
Cuz my fear has grown
My heart is broken
My anger burns on
Don't hug me although comfort you bring
I must be a soldier
No time to disengage
Head up, shoulders back
She needs me to be strong
Hugs can wait til later
Right now, man up and carry on

Mist Over The Pasture

Like a mist over the pasture
Your will lingers still
Despite uncertainty
You are still very real
I believe now help my unbelief
Lift the mist for me to see
What your future holds
Defeat or victory

I Need Your Wisdom

To figure this all out
I don't want to move and be in doubt
I need your wisdom
To handle all affairs
I know you are with me
I know you care
"I love you" I hear you whisper
"I'm proud of you too"
"I will give you wisdom"
"Just keep being you"

Calm Seas

As I sit early in the morning
Wondering how did this happen
I know beyond doubt
My ship has a captain
Most days I'm miserable
Lumps in my throat
Yet the captain of the seas still steers my boat
I know I don't deserve safe passage along the way
I know even when I'm distant and feeling some typa way
Your hand controls the helm
You calm the seas as well
I'm up early wanting to hear your voice
Cuz my heart is overwhelmed
Overwhelmed with gratitude
Cuz I do not deserve all you've done for me
In awe of your goodness and desire to set me free
I'm awake, alert, and open to what you'll speak to me
I'm honored to be loved and seen by the captain of calm seas...

Life Is My Muse

What should I write about
What can I say
Let's start with the love I feel every single day
Love from the Father constant and true
Love from my family even when it's not due
The peace in my home
Early morning silence I enjoy
The fact that we met
A wild little girl, a sweet shy boy
I could write about my job
Tough but well worth it
I could write about my co-workers
Boy are they worthy
I could write about my pain
Deep, lifelong disasters
I could write about my neighbors
And enjoying much laughter

I could write about my take on the world being a hot mess
I could write about how much I like sneakers
And heels so much less

These Words Just Got Me Through

I could make you laugh writing about our dog
Billy is his name
Bossy, bully but scared of everything all the same
I could write about my journey up steep hills, rough terrain
Would you still be reading
Will you remember my name